make:
CORNWALL

make:
CORNWALL

ANYA RICE &
KATHERINE SORRELL

First published in Great Britain in 2019 by Anya Rice and Katherine Sorrell

Maker photography © Anya Rice
Text © Katherine Sorrell
Landscape photography © Ben Mostyn
Front cover image © Paper Birch
Design: Peggy Sadler
Front cover design: Krystal Fanning
Proof-reader: Jo Godfrey Wood

ISBN 978-1-5272-4252-4
Printed by SS Media
◉ @makecornwallproject

Contents

Introduction

In this book we hope to shine a light on some of the most exciting, intriguing and inspirational makers working in Cornwall today.

Breathtaking scenery, vast skies and a unique quality of light have drawn artists to the far South West for more than two centuries, and the creative scene in Cornwall continues to thrive today. It is a hub of exceptional talent, home to makers who often incorporate the latest in modern technology while honouring age-old skills.

Cornwall is far from London and other metropolitan centres, and that can be a challenge, but it is also one of its strengths. From rugged coastlines to windswept moors, hidden woodlands to sub-tropical gardens, it is possible to feel intimately connected to nature here, with an unparalleled sense of space, together with the ability to think clearly and simply breathe deeply.

And while Cornwall may be far away, it is not left behind. The contemporary design coming from Cornwall is equal to anything coming from the capital or beyond. There is a focus on innovation, sustainability and working co-operatively that is genuinely exciting and, we believe, deserves greater exposure.

The quality and diversity of creative talent in Cornwall is extraordinary. For this book we have chosen 25 makers (though we could have selected many more) who represent a wide range of disciplines, including ceramics, textiles, weaving, glass art, leather work, paper craft and jewellery design. Some are at the very beginning of their careers; others have been in business for decades. Some are relatively undiscovered; others are selling globally through their websites or via prestigious national retailers. In many cases they have an intense focus on environmental awareness – living so close to the ocean, plastic waste, for example, is a constant concern. They are all part of a growing movement towards an appreciation of the hand-made, in which purposeful, considered, characterful objects connect the maker to the end user in a meaningful way. Their work is original and impressive, designed with flair and produced with absolute integrity. We love what they do, and we hope you will, too.

Anya   Katherine

Amy Isles Freeman

At the age of 19, Amy Isles Freeman had a feminist awakening. She was studying for a degree in drawing at Falmouth University and began to focus on communicating her new thoughts through art. Then she went to an exhibition of pieces by Dorothy Iannone (whose multi-media erotic art has been described as ornamental, figurative and folkish) and everything changed again. Amy realised that humour was the best communication tool and felt free to make work that would elicit smiles and laughter.

Amy initially had no desire to study in Cornwall and was dragged reluctantly to her course open day by her mother. From the moment she got off the train, however, she was drawn to the laid-back, coastal lifestyle, and when she graduated it was an easy decision to stay near Falmouth. She set up her studio in a converted piggery on a farm and, itching to learn a practical skill, asked her then-boyfriend to teach her how to use a lathe. It was another epiphany. Amy took to wood-turning and married it with her artistic practice, combining fine art and functional object, starting with simple decoration but quickly becoming more confident and intricate. Then, when an Instagram post of a work in progress led to the surprise offer of a stand at the London Design Fair, a viable business was born. Amy now spends time working in both Cornwall and Brighton, teaches workshops and has a growing product range that encompasses painted clothing, works on paper and, of course, decorative bowls, painted with bold, colourful patterns that celebrate female sexuality, freedom and pure joy.

UNION
JUBILEE

Above left Each of Amy's bowls is unique. Many celebrate femininity, while others depict flora and fauna, birds or tigers.

Left Amy works on an old Union Jubilee lathe, generally using beech wood, which has few knots and possesses a warm colour.

Above At one end of Amy's studio is her lathe, while the other is filled with painting equipment and a wall of colourful art cards.

Opposite Amy's mother was an illustrator who was influenced by American folk art, and Amy believes that the highly decorative patterns, naïve shapes and joyful colours that surrounded her as she grew up have been built into her own creative foundations.

Right Amy hand paints each bowl using acrylics paints. She finishes them with a hard-wearing, water-based floor varnish and protects the unpainted inside with a food-safe oil.

Below right The simple forms of Amy's hand-turned bowls contrast with their intricate decoration. They combine fine art, craft and illustration in a single object.

Wendy Wilbraham

Ceramics: art or craft? Wendy Wilbraham feels fortunate to have studied at Camberwell School of Arts and Crafts in the 80s, a pivotal time, when the historical traditions associated with tableware were re-examined. Having been taught by committed people who not only shared their skills but also encouraged searching conversation, she continues the debate through her thoughtful practice, making subtle vessel forms for everyday life, to hold and to use, but also to contemplate. When making her beakers, cups, dishes, bowls, pourers and bottles, Wendy tries to combine weight with lightness, conscious of balance, purpose and how her touch is translated into each piece.

For Wendy, who works from a spare room in her 17th-century townhouse in Penryn, the necessity to make something is closely linked with drawing: quick graphite sketches or sumptuous, coloured-ink meanderings, exploring ideas and feelings. As she throws on the wheel, she tries to guide her thoughts into the clay; later, she may cut facets with wire or inscribe sgraffito lines. Her glazing is often in white (matt and shiny) or blue: it is the final process that, she believes, transforms the ware into an object that awakens the senses. Wendy is inspired by many things, from the work of Lucy Rie and Giorgio Morandi to Japanese ikat weaving, discordant music, folded piles of fabric and the greys of Cornwall's slate, granite and cloudy weather. Living here, she appreciates the backdrop of discovery and innovation, the integrated community, the absolute beauty of the surroundings, the occasional busyness and the welcome quiet.

Opposite As Wendy throws she is conscious of lightness and weight, of balance and purpose.

Above and above right The making of each form begins with a ball of clay and a wheel, some water, a sponge and a few well-favoured tools. Once thrown, some of the pieces are cut with a wire to create facets.

Right Wendy's sketches are a necessary part of her process. She works in soft graphite pencil and coloured inks.

Below right
Experiments with colour in Wendy's studio. For her terracotta ware, she uses porcelain slip as a bright grounding for transparent, coloured earthenware glazes.

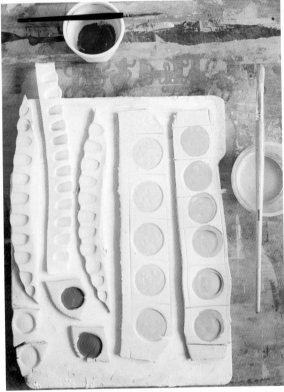

Above An array of time-honoured, traditional tools, which are both familiar and reliable.

Below In the studio, a jumble of much-loved items adorns the walls, shelves and peg rails.

Below right Buckets containing a variety of glazes, each designed through an exacting process of blending carefully calculated raw materials.

Opposite Wendy's making process draws greatly on her drawings. She enjoys working on long, narrow paper that, for her, conforms to the iterative process of making ceramics.

Rose Choules

Rose Choules is fascinated by traditional hand-work, the everyday craft of everyday people that springs from necessity, showing self sufficiency and a connection to the natural world. And she has always been intrigued by moccasins, an ancient style that is both utilitarian and rich in cultural symbolism; plain and simple on the one hand, but also embellished and individually expressive.

Having studied footwear design and completed a fashion degree, Rose worked for many years as a shoe designer in the fashion industry, but it was, perhaps, inevitable that she would find her way back to hand-making shoes. In 2011 she won a footwear design award that gave her the opportunity to set up a pop-up moccasin atelier in the Selfridges shoe galleries in London, where she offered a ready-to-wear collection and stitched bespoke styles for customers. Soon after, she visited Northern Saskatchewan in Canada to share skills with Cree artisans, returning home with some home-smoked moose hide, rare beads and a plan to also develop a baby moccasin collection.

Today, based in a spare room in her home in Bude, Rose makes women's and baby moccasins, handbags, purses and other accessories, using a variety of soft suedes, rhubarb-tanned leather, felt from Dartmoor sheep and hand-woven or printed fabrics. Her pieces, which blend traditional techniques with a sustainable ethos and modern aesthetic, often incorporate rare or vintage trims, original beadwork designs and small, hand-stitched details. Rose runs regular workshops with children and adults, too, sharing her satisfaction in creating leather goods of use and joy.

Above Pieces of leather or suede are carefully cut and then holes punched, where necessary, before they are sewn together.

Above right Rose uses a 1940s post-bed sewing machine, which produces very fine stitching.

Opposite Everything that Rose makes is from an original design, starting out as a sketch and then transferred onto card patterns, which are cut out with as little waste as possible produced.

Right Debossing the distinctive Rose Choules logo onto leather, using a manual press.

Below right Rose enjoys using different types of stitching and seams. These cross-stitched leather tassels are a signature of her work.

Above Rose's studio, in the spare room of her home in Bude.

Left Both traditional and modern hand tools are used in the making of Rose's products.

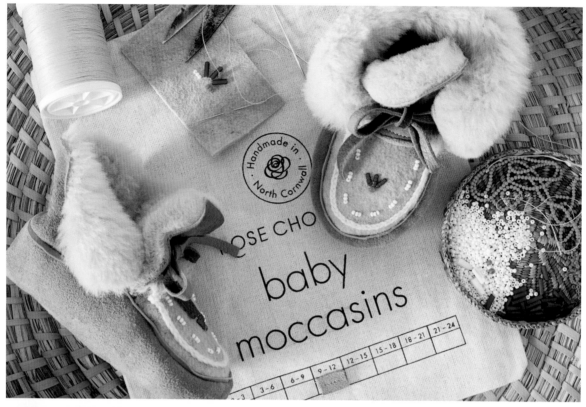

Above Bespoke baby moccasins may employ a variety of decorative techniques, such as Japanese sashiko stitching and fine beadwork.

Left Inspired by hand-work from many different cultures and times, including royal shoemakers John Lobb and the Cree artisans of northern Canada, Rose tries to balance the utilitarian and the decorative in everything she makes.

Opposite Rose works with rhubarb-tanned leather and high-quality suedes from a specialist supplier, in an array of colours.

Alice Selwood

Embroidery designer Alice Selwood works in the luxury fashion and interiors market, specialising in creating elegant and detailed digital embellishment on bags, cushions, lampshades and other products. Since graduating from Falmouth University in 2015, she has won a number of awards, collaborated with Gingerlily silk bedlinen to become an Art Partner with Harrods (putting her in the company of Dolce & Gabbana, Wedgwood and Missoni) and rapidly developed a global business. She is based in a converted barn on a small farm just outside Redruth, and everything she makes is sourced within the UK, with local craftspeople helping out when necessary.

Alice's inspirations are Cornwall's industrial heritage and natural landscapes, from textures and patterns encountered on walks on the beach or in the countryside to the dramatic structures of mining engineering and the colours of rock minerals. From the sketches she produces while exploring the Cornish countryside, Alice painstakingly develops digital design files that are stitched by 'Happy', her state-of-the-art 15-needle embroidery machine. Her sophisticated designs – textural, bold, geometric and often vibrantly coloured – push the boundaries of traditional embroidery and explore the potential for extending this age-old skill into the 21st century.

Above Inspired by the strong structures of mining engineering, the designs in this collection are bold, geometric and highly textured.

Above right Alice's digital embroidery machine, 'Happy', is capable of producing 1,000 stitches per minute.

Opposite After graduating from university, Alice won an award that provided her with design software and a sponsored embroidery machine, enabling her to continue designing for herself.

Opposite Alice's sketches – often made on walks in the Cornish countryside – are the starting-off point for her work.

Above The shelves of the studio are stacked with graphic, colourful products, ranging from tiny coin purses to large cushions and lampshades.

Paper Birch

For Krystal Fanning, the process is just as beautiful as the end product. Inspired by wandering Cornwall's quiet woodlands, sub-tropical gardens and breathtaking coastlines, she produces a range of stationery and lifestyle products, including art prints, note cards and custom pieces.

Krystal studied fine art, photography and multi-media in Dorset, where she grew up, then came to Cornwall to do a degree in graphic design at Falmouth University. She never left, working first for a leading Cornish design agency and then for herself, setting up her creative lifestyle brand, Paper Birch, at her home studio in Penryn. Nature and plants are her inspirations, and it is while on a country stroll or shoreline walk that her designs take shape, as she collects beautiful examples of foliage, flowers and seaweed to transform into hand-made silhouette impressions. Krystal uses a photographic printing technique called cyanotype, invented by Sir John Herschel in 1842, in which she paints light-sensitive emulsion onto paper, composes her subjects on top and exposes the work in the sunlight. Washing the print results in a cyan-blue chemical reaction, and these indigo-rich artworks are the basis for Paper Birch's products, their unique botanical patterns and textures combining with carefully chosen papers and typefaces to capture what is natural and special about a particular place.

Opposite Krystal collects promising foliage – in this case, palm fronds – from her own garden and on regular walks in the countryside.

Left Before arranging foliage, flowers or seaweed on the paper, Krystal paints it with a chemical emulsion, which starts off green but becomes blue when exposed to UV light.

Below left The chemical emulsion is washed off in a tray of water.

Overleaf The cyanotype exposures are hung in the sun to dry.

Right and below right
Krystal uses her
cyanotypes as a basis
for bespoke designs
and her ranges of
printed stationery and
lifestyle products.

Opposite A neat corner
of Krystal's studio in her
home in Penryn.

Glass by Bryony

With shining, textured glass and coloured shadows, Bryony Lane aims to bring the beauty of plants and nature into a room. She is passionate about stained glass, believing that it can capture something about our ever-changing lives, the seasons, trees and plants, the weather and the sea. Trained as a graphic designer, Bryony worked at a desk in Brighton for years before moving to Falmouth and setting up her business, Glass by Bryony, taking a short course run by stained-glass professionals, plus some online tutorials to teach herself further skills. She now works from her garden-shed studio, inspired by the flowers, foliage, seaweeds and landscapes nearby, as well as the designs of Victorian stained-glass doors and the colours and textures of the vintage glass that is a particular characteristic of her roundels and panels.

Bryony's starting point is a freehand drawing, often based on her photographs of a particular botanical feature. Many of her works use rare off-cuts of German mouth-blown glass, which possess irregular streaks and bubbles and provide a starting point for her choices of the other glass pieces with which to surround them – sometimes punchy and contrasting in colour, sometimes quietly naturalistic. Bryony uses Tiffany techniques, foiling the edges of the cut glass with copper strip and soldering them together with lead, but although her methods are rooted in tradition, her work is notably clean-lined, fresh and strikingly current.

Above A fern roundel in progress. A similar piece was shortlisted for the 2018 Liberty Open Call.

Right After cutting each piece of glass, it has to be ground around the edges to make it smooth, then it is washed and numbered. Bryony sticks copper foil around the edges, burnishes the foil and solders everything together.

Below right Using the Tiffany technique allows Bryony to produce complex, curved designs with strong, graphic shapes.

Below left Bryony
feels that bright,
transparent glass
and the movement of
its coloured shadows
can offer a sense of
grounding.

Below right Having
drawn her design,
quickly and freehand,
Bryony carefully
chooses the glass
that will give the most
pleasing results, then
cuts it accurately.

Sarah Drew

Every day, Sarah Drew goes to the beach near her St Austell workshop and collects curious things: perhaps some colourful beach plastic, a flat slate pebble, some sea glass, a delicate shell, a length of abandoned fishing net or a lump of driftwood. They are all to be used for her statement jewellery, in which she combines found materials with eco-silver, recycled brass and gold, and sustainable semi-precious stones. It is obvious at a glance how much the Cornish landscape – from open beaches and shifting seas, to rock textures and post-industrial scenery – directly influences Sarah's work. She also loves mid-century design and is inspired by Barbara Hepworth's organic sculptures, as well as the muted-bright colour palettes of artists Terry Frost, Peter Lanyon, Margaret Mellis and Sandra Blow.

Sarah has been making jewellery since she was 14, but did a degree in communications and worked in retail management before setting up her business, picking up further skills via an evening class, books, helpful jewellers and online videos. She makes her metals look ancient and interesting by fusing, casting, hammering, scratching and oxidising them, and many of her tools and techniques are traditional. However, because some of her materials can't be heated and are difficult to drill, she has also developed a variety of creative ways to connect different elements. These include crochet, threading and 'stitching' with wire, as well as riveting and glueing. The result is an eclectic range of unique and sustainable pieces that challenge our conception of what makes something precious.

Right Sarah searches for sea glass and other curious objects washed up on her local beaches, filling her pockets with her finds.

Below right Treasures stored in Sarah's St Austell workshop, ready to be assembled into unique and beautiful pieces of jewellery.

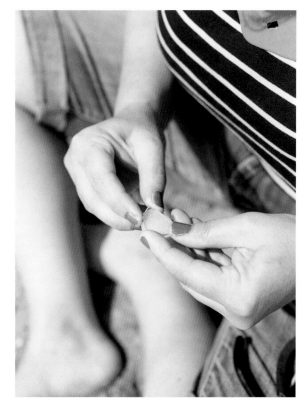

Left Sawing a small piece of silver on the bench peg.

Below left Fusing, casting, hammering, scratching and oxidising are all methods used to create an aged and interesting finish to Sarah's eco-silver and recycled brass and gold.

Below right Metal pieces can be soldered, but some of Sarah's jewellery employs unconventional joining methods such as crochet or 'stitching' with wire.

Opposite Sarah lays out the pieces she has found to decide how they will best combine.

Above Striking jewellery made with sea plastic, crocheted sea string and eco-silver, some fused and oxidised.

Left The influence of mid-century artists such as Barbara Hepworth, Terry Frost and Peter Lanyon can be seen in the organic shapes of Sarah's pieces.

Otter Surfboards

Otter Surfboards was born from James Otter's twin passions: fine woodworking and surfing. It was during his Designer Maker degree at Plymouth University that he read a magazine article about wooden surfboards and had a eureka moment: a lifelong surfer, he realised that he wanted to make boards that were both durable and environmentally friendly. He began developing his ideas, then set up business in Porthtowan, on Cornwall's north coast, soon after graduating. Only a year or so later, he was approached by someone who wanted to learn how to make his own board – and from there the Otter workshops began, in which customers (not necessarily with any experience in woodworking) enrol on an intensive, week-long course to make the surfboard of their dreams. James now combines making and teaching, which he finds hugely rewarding.

Otter's surfboards combine traditional materials with modern refinements and construction methods, with a strong focus on how to make the least environmental impact. James uses red cedar and poplar sustainably grown in the South West, along with hardwood offcuts from a local kitchen worktop company. He builds each board around an internal frame, carefully assembling it so as to make the most of the timber's natural grain and patterning. They are laminated by a specialist in nearby Wadebridge, using bio-epoxy resins and fibreglass cloth, before being polished up to a glassy sheen – ready for their first dip in the ocean.

Above Sustainably
grown red cedar is
combined with salvaged
hardwood offcuts to
become panels for the
bottom and deck skins
of the surfboards.

Opposite James is
based in a workshop
in the Mount Pleasant
Eco Park, a sustainable
community space set
in 42 acres of organic
farmland on the north
Cornish coast.

Above Once the hollow surfboard blank has been constructed, the rails are carefully shaped.

Right While the internal frames of the boards are cut by a computer-controlled router, much of the work is completed using traditional hand tools.

Below right James makes wooden hollow skin and frame boards, inspired by the construction techniques pioneered by legendary surfboard designer Tom Blake in the 1930s.

Above The internal frames – which look like fish skeletons – are cut, assembled and glued onto the bottom skin. Then, rail strips made of poplar are built up around the ribs, and the deck skin is glued on top.

Left James stamps his logo on every finished product.

Overleaf A row of beautiful hand-crafted boards is lined up outside the Otter workshop.

Francli

Ali Goodman is a firm believer in purpose-led design. Her good-looking workwear and accessories are, first and foremost, functional and durable, inspired by timeless, practical styles from the past and the adventurous makers in her own creative community. Francli products are solutions to problems, often created in collaboration – like the Leach potter's apron, developed over months of testing with workers at the Leach Pottery in St Ives. Ali specialises in personalised rucksacks for outdoor enthusiasts and aprons for craft businesses, each item a reliable, long-lasting and resilient companion.

Having studied performance sportswear design at Falmouth University and had a stint working as a fashion intern in London, Ali returned to Cornwall and now works in a former cattle shed, part of a creative business community based on a farm just outside Falmouth. Surrounded by beautiful countryside, she is completely connected with nature and the outdoors, and committed to sustainable, ethical, socially aware design. She sources materials based on her concern for the growing wastefulness of the fashion and outdoor industries, frequently salvaging and re-appropriating would-be-wasted products such as army surplus, discontinued climbing equipment and boat factory off-cuts, while much of her webbing, thread, waxed cotton and hardware is made in the UK. It's about reducing environmental impact, integrity, working with the hands, being considered... slow fashion that is the absolute opposite of the modern throwaway culture.

Above Francli was initially planned as a three-month project with a friend. This blue 1930s Singer flatbed sewing machine was their first purchase for the venture.

Above right Ali makes bespoke pieces, as one-offs and in small batches, which are tailored to specific crafts, businesses and environments.

Right A modular, moveable stand with pegs and shelves is a simple and effective way to store and display.

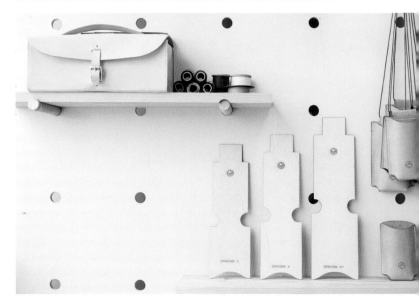

Right The phone/
card case, made from
vegetable-tanned
leather, has been a core
Francli product since
the beginning.

Below right Ali designs
hardy workwear and
outdoor accessories for
creators and explorers.

Opposite and above
Francli is based in a studio at Argal Home Farm, near Falmouth, where like-minded practices work alongside each other – with beautiful views of the Cornish countryside.

Left In hard-wearing waxed canvas, cotton twill and re-purposed surplus canvas, the made-to-order Outdoor Smock (on the right) is, like all Francli products, hugely practical and made to last.

Dor & Tan

Family members Sharron, Peter and Matt, plus close friend Viola, make up Hayle-based pottery studio Dor & Tan (meaning 'earth and fire' in Cornish). They focus on minimal, contemporary forms with strong purpose and function – pieces that will pass the test of time and earn a place in people's lives.

Each member of the group has different skills and responsibilities. While everyone works in the studio, wedging the clay, throwing smaller items and glazing, it is Sharron (who has a degree in 3D ceramic design and 40 years of experience as a potter), who designs all the ceramics and throws most of them. Peter, with extensive knowledge of finance and business strategy, gets things moving in the right direction. Matt, a trained scientist, helps with glaze development and runs the website, while Viola is in charge of photography and branding.

Inspiration comes from all sorts of areas: minimal architecture, wild plants, Japanese and Korean pottery, modern and classic design and, of course, the rugged beauty of the Cornish environment. All four are avid nature explorers, with a soft spot for the coastline around St Ives and St Agnes – full of wildlife, lichens and rock forms. Sustainability is a core element of Dor & Tan's design philosophy: their stoneware clay is sourced locally, wedged by hand, thrown primarily using kick wheels, fired in kilns powered by energy from renewables and sent out in recyclable packaging. Their aim? To make things thoughtfully; the proper way rather than the easy way.

Opposite Sharron throwing at the wheel, which is powered by green energy.

Right Peter, finance and business expert, lends a hand with wedging up the clay. Like kneading dough, this process makes the clay pliable and uniform, and gets rid of trapped air bubbles.

Below A series of colourful glaze tests alongside some finished pieces in the corner of the studio.

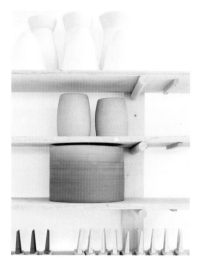

Above Thrown pieces are left on the shelves to dry before they can be fired and glazed.

Right Every member of the team helps with glazing. Here, Viola and Matt are dipping a batch of espresso cups in a yellow glaze.

Below right and opposite Dor & Tan's espresso cups in their gorse-yellow glaze – inspired by walks along the coast of Cornwall, where, in spring and summer, an abundance of spiky gorse, with its vividly coloured and gently scented flowers, is to be found.

Opposite Iron-rich clay creates subtle speckling under a soft celadon glaze, inspired by the lichen-encrusted rocks and misty green horizons seen on walks on the coastal path between Gwithian and St Agnes.

Left The pristine studio, which is flooded with light from all sides.

Below left Stamped on the bottom of each piece, the name Dor & Tan means 'earth and fire' in Cornish.

Sea of Grass

Donna Jonas' business was a natural development of her interest in ecology and sustainability. A creative person since childhood, as an adult she worked in stone masonry and carving, developed a small business making paper, and painted cards and prints using her own vibrant, hand-made paints. And when she wanted her children to have safe, natural art materials for creative projects, she began to explore natural earth and plant-dye pigments. Donna made up a variety of colours, in mini jam jars from a local café – and Sea of Grass was born.

Donna's raw materials (sourced from small, eco-friendly suppliers) come from all corners of the earth, which is reflected in the name Sea of Grass – a prairie on the plains of Ukraine many millennia ago, where Asian, Celtic and European cultures came together. Her products include beeswax crayons and watercolours in jars, tubes and tins, as well as recycled-paper sketchbooks with fair-trade African bark-cloth covers. Made by Donna in her studio in Boscastle, the paints and crayons are free from chemicals, fillers, binders and driers, and have a lovely depth and purity of colour. No two batches are the same: each pigment behaves differently and she has to feel her way every time, but ultimately the process is hugely satisfying. As Donna sees it, her work is a contribution towards a simpler, more sustainable, slower way of living.

Opposite Donna's paints are hand-made in small batches using simple ingredients and processes.

Above A few of the pigments, created by what Donna describes as 'green, sustainable chemistry', that are the base for her natural art materials.

Left Donna fills small glass jars (easily recyclable) with the watercolour paint that she has mixed.

Above Donna melts beeswax to create non-toxic crayons.

Right Constantly thinking about sustainability, Donna has designed packaging that is minimal and easily recyclable.

Below right Sea of Grass watercolour paints are UV-resistant, non-toxic, vibrant and free-flowing, with a notable depth and purity of colour.

Above Donna's beeswax crayons come in a range of earth and bright colours.

Juniper Bespoke

A bookbinder, writer, playwright, illustrator, designer and printmaker, Emily Juniper collaborates with clients to create books that are made to be loved, used and touched by the passage of time. Her work has included a story to help a child to understand loss, a way of keeping recipes written on the backs of envelopes, and a marriage proposal in the form of a book (the answer was yes).

Emily grew up in a house that was lined with books, did a literature degree, then trained as an actor. She has been a magician's assistant, a corporate receptionist, a copywriter and a dancer, and the bespoke books came about after encouragement from her brother, when she read him a book that she had made for a friend. After starting a business in Camberwell, London, she moved to Falmouth to do the university's MA in illustration and authorial practice, and within six months had decided to stay. A chance comment led to her renting her studio on the high street, a former shop with space in front for a book display and her equipment, and a back room where Emily is often be found intensely focusing on her work.

Emily approaches each book as a kind of theatre. She thinks of the opening of a book as being like the raising of the curtain, and selecting a font like casting an actor based on their tone of voice. She can spend days choosing just the right white paper, and loves how binding involves both mathematical precision and creativity, with the finished product a combination of carefully chosen elements that seduce the reader.

Right The choice of exactly the right coloured thread is essential when Emily hand-stitches a binding.

Below right Emily uses a hacksaw to create a series of regular holes in the folded edges of the paper, ready for stitching.

Opposite Though from the outside it looks like a shop, the studio is actually a working space in which Emily can become absorbed in each project.

Above and right The prize money from winning a bookbinding competition gave Emily the opportunity to study letterpress printing. She fell in love with it and now collects old letterpress equipment, including these drawers full of metal type.

Below right One of Emily's favourite methods of bookbinding is a linking stitch (as shown on the book at the bottom), which allows a book to lie flat when it is opened.

Opposite Emily has filled her studio with objects that are meaningful for her.

Left Essential
equipment: an old
wooden book clamp, a
50-year-old typewriter
and a yellow vintage
Adana three-five
lever press.

Below Emily's studio on
Falmouth's High Street.
She enjoys creating
an intriguing window
display.

Opposite Ranks of past
projects by Juniper
Bespoke demonstrate
Emily's approach – to
create unique books
that tempt the reader
to take them down from
the shelf.

Our faces, composed
(with discretionary
ligatures) await a kiss.

OEDIPA

De-Vey

née

Our faces, composed
(with discretionary
ligatures) await a kiss.

Pica Pica

Resourcefulness and sustainability are at the heart of Claire Thorp's creative process. It starts with her scouring junk shops, vintage fairs and local beaches for delicate and interesting components to include in her range of understated, eco-conscious jewellery – hence her company's name, which means 'magpie' in Latin.

Claire's formal training was in textile design, followed by working for print and fashion studios in London, and then as a stylist in New York. A chance meeting at a flea market in Brooklyn led to a job working for a jeweller and, eventually, Claire brought together her skills, her appreciation of colour and texture and her love of finding beauty in the old, the worn and the unexpected, to form Pica Pica.

Instead of following a formal, planned process, Claire works by setting out her gathered objects – anything from shells and beads to antique necklace chains and old fishing floats – on her desk and allowing them to guide her, intuitively responding to how she feels each piece wants to be. Her favourite elements are those that evoke a sense of resilience, of having survived against the odds. She enjoys giving them renewed purpose, sanding, painting, rearranging and reworking them to transform them into bespoke items of jewellery that juxtapose their weathered textures with a clean, minimal and modern aesthetic. A selection of hand-made greetings cards in recycled paper complements Claire's jewellery range.

Opposite Pica Pica jewellery juxtaposes the weathered colours and intriguing textures of vintage and found items with a clean, modern, minimal aesthetic.

Below left A selection of 'findings', the additional elements such as clasps, jump rings and fasteners used to create functional jewellery.

Below right When making her pieces, Claire assembles the components on her desk and pieces them together in an intuitive way, guided by shapes, colours and textures.

Above Claire strings a selection of repurposed beads, chosen for their beautiful shapes and colours, onto unbleached cotton cord.

Right Claire chose the name 'Pica Pica', meaning 'magpie' in Latin, because she is constantly on the lookout for interesting components with which to make her jewellery.

Below right Although she works with found and vintage items, Claire uses traditional jewellery tools and techniques.

Right and below right A greetings card line made using 100% recycled paper complements the Pica Pica jewellery range. Each card is hand-drawn by Claire, who once worked in print and fashion studios in London.

Ondine Ash

Ondine Ash's eponymous business came about after she spent 16 years working as a buyer in the fashion industry. She loved travelling the world and her job gave her a unique insight into how, where and by whom things are made. When she decided to take a break, it was a natural step to launch an ethically conscious homeware collection, initially online only, with a mission to move away from fast, throwaway fashion and focus on transparency. Her partner's desire to return to Cornwall with their young family brought them to Falmouth, where Ondine was able to set up a bricks-and-mortar shop-cum-studio in Old Brewery Yard, a thriving, fashionable area of the historic coastal town.

In a corner of the shop, where she sells ceramics, candles, blankets and other items that are produced fairly and responsibly, Ondine has set up a sewing machine and overlocker, so that she can work between serving customers. Inspired by the textiles and traditional forms of dress that she encountered while exploring Africa, India, Japan and Latin America, and fostered by a love of sewing that she developed at a young age, she makes cushions using mud cloth (hand-printed using fermented mud in bold patterns) from Mali, and hanging baskets from cotton cord that she hand-dyes with natural indigo. While still early days, the move from the virtual world to the real one has been positive so far, and Ondine has found that having a space where she can make, sell, meet new people and be part of the community has been a total joy.

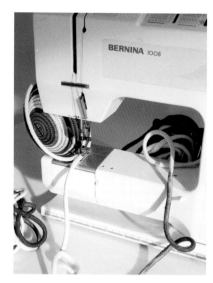

Above Inspired by coil pottery, Ondine sculpts baskets – that she later lines with plastic, so they can hold plant pots – from about 16 metres of hand-dyed cord, zig-zag stitched together.

Right As well as making mud-cloth cushions, Ondine also designs a range of organic cotton cushions that are produced ethically for her in a small factory in India.

Below right The sewing machine is set up in the corner of the shop, where Ondine sells her own products and other hand-made, ethically sourced, pieces.

Above Above Ondine's baskets hang alongside displays of ceramics, including earthenware made in the UK by Sue Pryke.

Kelmi

All the rage in the 70s, then out in the wilderness for decades, macramé is back in fashion with a bang. The art of making textiles from knotting dates back many hundreds of years – and while it is an inherently simple process, there is a wealth of different knots and patterns that may be employed, and the possibilities for this traditional craft are endless.

The potential offered by macramé is just one of the reasons why Zaya Gilchrist and Lucy Skuse started their business, Kelmi, which means 'to tie' or 'to bind' in Cornish. Friends living in Falmouth, who met when their children started at the same school, they both completed creative degrees but ended up working in education. With a shared love of making, they wanted to learn a new skill and, drawn to the symmetry and simplicity of macramé, as well as the therapeutic nature of its repetitive movements, began to develop designs together. Kelmi products – all made in Zaya's attic workspace – range from small decorations to large wall hangings, including plant and tea-light holders, bunting, lampshades and wedding arches. Using cotton yarns from British companies and wood sourced from the abundant beaches and woodlands of Cornwall, Zaya and Lucy are inspired not only by the symmetry and patterns of nature, but also by art movements such as the Bauhaus and Arts and Crafts, and aim to offer an antidote to mass-produced items as well as a unique, eco-friendly alternative for consumers.

Above Kelmi's natural wood hangings are sourced from Cornish woodlands.

Left Zaya developing pattern ideas at her desk under the skylight.

Opposite Lucy works on a new plant hanger design.

Opposite Designs start with a pattern sketch, but tend to evolve once Lucy and Zaya start knotting.

Below left The raw materials and tools for macramé are simple: yarn, scissors, measuring tape… and dextrous hands.

Below right Kelmi products are made from cotton yarns of different thicknesses and colours, all from British companies.

Above The studio is in the attic of Zaya's townhouse in Falmouth. Products range from tiny, decorative pieces to large wall hangings, lampshades and even wedding arches.

Opposite A row of plant hangers demonstrates just a few of the range of knots and patterns that can be produced.

Tinkebu

Tucked away in a small workshop next to his home in Truro, Jaime Tinker creates a rainbow of tractors, campervans and land yachts, baby gyms and cuddly rockers, foot stools and pull-alongs, each creation slightly different from the next and with its own unique character.

Jaime grew up around woodworking, never happier than when playing about in the garage with his father and brother. He took a few evening classes in his twenties, gaining carpentry and joinery qualifications at Truro and Penwith College, all the while making and upcycling furniture for his home. However, it wasn't until he decided to put together a few toys and items of furniture as gifts for friends and family that Tinkebu was born. The presents were enthusiastically received and Jaime's hobby quickly turned into a business.

In an age of ever-increasing throwaway plastic, Tinkebu does things more responsibly. Traditional with a modern twist, the range uses only reclaimed and sustainably sourced materials: wood from local salvage yards, hand-painted in non-toxic, attractive colours, and with the occasional addition of ethical Dartmoor sheepskin. And in a partnership with global reforestation charity One Tree Planted, every time he sells a product Jamie also plants a tree. Neat.

Opposite For each batch of products, Jaime has to select and clean the right piece of salvaged wood before measuring and cutting.

Right As much as possible, everything is made using hand tools, giving each item a unique character.

Below right To finish his products, Jaime uses only certified non-toxic paints and waxes.

Above As well as the small pull-alongs, Jaime also makes larger toys, such as Hamish, the Highland cow rocker.

Right Jaimie's business started after his first child arrived. Reluctant to buy into the overwhelming tide of garish plastic, he began to make wooden toys for her.

Below right There is always something waiting on Jaime's workbench.

Above Jaime's designs
are inspired by
Cornwall; his traditional
wooden toys relate
in theme to farming,
tourism and the sea.

Deer & Shine

When Abi Wason started making jewellery, she felt as if a light had been switched back on in her brain. It was a sensation of being completely absorbed in her work, totally in the present. A winding path led her eventually to this point. After an upbringing filled with art and craft, followed by a degree in media and visual arts, she worked as a graphic and web designer, freelance photographer, BBC journalist and teacher of baby swimming – and her change of direction came about when a good friend (and professional jeweller) offered Abi one-to-one silversmithing lessons. Despite work and three young children, she was yearning to make again, so found the time and quickly gained the necessary skills, then started to experiment on her own.

With leftover timber from a home extension, Abi built a wendy house in the garden for her children (not a spirit level in sight, but at least 750,000 nails, as she puts it) – and decided to turn it into a workshop from which to run her new business, Deer & Shine. She is based near the small town of St Just, on the furthest, wildest, western tip of Cornwall, and is fiercely inspired by the ever-changing landscapes, the weather patterns, the line of the horizon, symmetry and shapes in general. Geometry plays a big part in her work, and her pieces feature clean, sleek and minimal lines and angles, in silver, gold and brass, and sometimes with gemstones, crystals and feathers. Edgy, yet elegant, they combine contemporary and classic to arresting effect.

Right Abi works in silver, brass and gold, and is especially drawn to brass, enjoying the natural tarnishing process (which can be polished away) that makes the piece seem as if it is ever-changing.

Below right Making a Cascade necklace involves hammering numerous brass droplets to create a waterfall effect, and then threading them onto a necklet.

Opposite Some of Abi's finished pieces displayed in a vintage printer's tray in her workshop.

Left Foxy the cat sometimes sneaks in to watch Abi, perching on the bench among finished jewellery and work in progress.

Below Abi built her garden workshop by hand, using timber left over from creating a home extension.

Above Abi uses traditional silver-smithing techniques, including sawing, hammering and soldering. She likes to play with different materials, laying them out and assessing their qualities and how they relate to one another.

Left Inside Abi's shed is an assortment of items that she has gathered over the years.

Miel Studio

Miel Studio started out as a collaboration between friends and soon turned into a business venture. Ruth Haughton studied fashion design before going into teaching and moving to Spain, then relocated to Cornwall, lured by the beaches, the creativity and the slower pace of life. Holly Hearn – whose family has an antiquarian book business in Penzance – took a degree in culture and media studies, and started her first business in Bristol, producing cards that promoted the work of young artists. After eight years she decided to move back to Cornwall and met up with Ruth, whose partner was an old friend. The two women realised that they had a great deal in common, not least that both loved everything to do with paper and had recently been learning bookbinding.

Colour and pattern are passions for Holly and Ruth, but they appreciate subtlety and simplicity, too, and love combining some of the traditional processes of bookbinding with fresh, modern designs. For their paper goods brand, Miel Studio, they design and make tactile, desirable, functional products for people and their desks, aimed at helping the buyer lead a creative life – pastel-coloured artist portfolios, letter-writing sets, hand-bound sketchbooks wrapped in ribbon, wrapping paper and hot-foiled notecards and tags. They find inspiration in the everyday – perhaps the pattern in a tiled wall, or a symbol in an old book, as well as in their extensive collections of art and design books – and especially enjoy the process of carefully placing together paper, book cloth and ribbon to create appealing colour combinations and a cohesive range of designs.

Above left Ruth at work on the foil press. Paper has always been a passion for her, and in her spare time she used to make hand-illustrated, concertina books.

Above right Colour and pattern are a constant source of inspiration for Ruth and Holly.

Left Many of Miel Studio's products are made using their vintage hot-foil press.

Opposite Holly moved back to Cornwall after eight years in Bristol because she felt it was a great place to start a creative business.

Above and opposite below Miel's range of paper goods displayed on shelves in Ruth and Holly's studio.

Opposite above Miel's portfolios are made from grey board and the brand's signature coloured papers, with contrasting book cloth for the spines and a length of cotton or linen ribbon to wrap around twice.

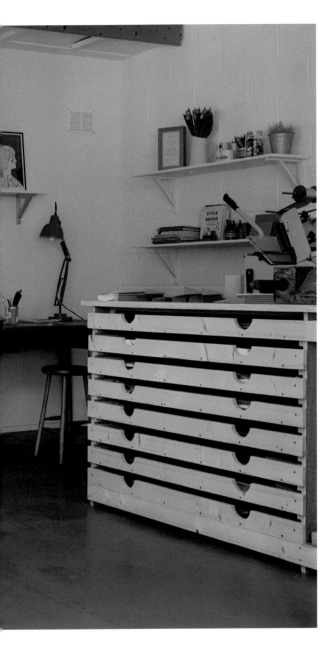

Ink Splat Notebooks - Black / White
2 x Lined notebooks // Recycled Grey Card

Opposite Ruth and Holly are inspired by the simple, tactile beauty of a piece of paper and make stationery to help people live creatively.

Left Holly attaches the ribbon that wraps twice around each portfolio.

Below left
A changing selection of inspirational imagery on the wall of the studio.

Lancaster & Cornish

Sian Lancaster is following in the footsteps of centuries of artisans who have harvested colour from nature. What she didn't know until years after she set up her business, Lancaster & Cornish, was that working with textiles is in her blood. Her great-grandfather was a Lancashire cotton weaver who, with her grandfather, set up a three-floor emporium in central Manchester in the 1920s and 30s, selling fabrics from around the world. Sian herself studied earth sciences at Oxford University and worked as an environmental consultant in the construction industry for years, until a move to Lostwithiel with her husband inspired a rethink. A trip to the Himalayas while studying for her Masters degree had deepened her love for colour, texture and fabrics, and Sian decided to follow her passion, with an ethos of keeping it intimate, ethical and kind to the environment.

Sian began experimenting with making dyes from fruit and vegetables, petals, plants and berries, boiling them up on her kitchen hob. Through trial and error she developed a palette of soft colours – that she now expands on each season. These days she works from a small shed in her garden, creating hand-dyed, luxurious ribbons, table linens and wedding textiles. She buys some natural dyes from fair-trade sources, but makes many herself from plants, flowers and seaweeds that she forages or grows; her textiles are inextricably linked to the Cornish landscape. She works on a small scale and feels an affinity with every piece she makes, pointing out that naturally dyed fabric has inimitable depth, subtlety and shading, a living colour that tells a truly authentic story.

Above Dyed ribbons hung to dry in Sian's workshop. She makes many of her dyes from flowers and petals that she forages herself.

Opposite above A corner of Sian's workshop shed. The bowls are used for small batches of dyeing by hand.

Opposite below Sian collecting gorse from a nearby hedge. She uses the flowers to make a beautifully clear yellow dye.

NCASTER
ORNISH
tiful organic fabric

Above Each ribbon, some of which have carefully hand-frayed edges, is spooled onto a sustainable wooden reel for safe-keeping.

Right Sian spends much time testing her colours. Once she has developed her secret recipe, she immerses each piece of silk or bamboo fabric individually in a dye bath.

Below right Natural dyes produce an intriguing range of living colours that are completely different to harsh, flat, commercial dyes.

Opposite Sian brushes pure gold, silver or copper leaf onto some ribbons and other products.

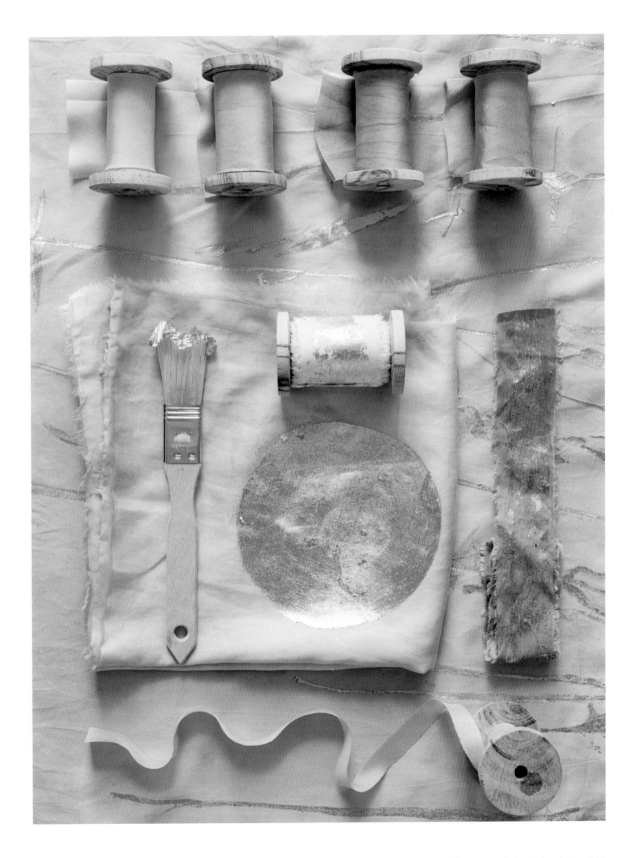

Studio Haran

Combining minimal style with natural materials, Joel and Helena Haran design and make luxury furniture, lighting and homewares from slip-cast ceramic and wood. They are based in a light-filled, white-painted former cattle shed on a farm near Mylor – and really do work to the sound of the lowing of cows.

Having met (and married) on the sustainable product design degree course at Falmouth University, Joel and Helena operate very much as a partnership. While Joel concentrates on woodwork and Helena on ceramics, they are both multi-disciplined and collaborate on every design decision, from pencil sketch to prototype to elegantly detailed finished piece. Their range spans chairs, stools and tables, hanging planters, chopping boards and a collection of lamps that unite both timber and ceramics, the latter in subtle colours and finishes that are inspired by the landscapes of Cornwall.

At the heart of Studio Haran's business is respect for the environment, with each product designed to last and with end-of-life disassembly in mind. Materials are sourced ethically: timber from either sustainably managed British woodland or that which is Forest Stewardship Council certified, and English earthenware and stoneware clay. The couple's craft processes are, on the whole, time-honoured and traditional, but their tactile products, which hint at Scandinavian purity and economy of line, are both modern and timeless – classic, but with a contemporary (and environmentally friendly) twist.

Above Joel bought many of his chisels online or at car boot sales, and others were inherited from Helena's grandfather, Bill.

Left Chopping boards and a Sennen table lamp on the workbench, in front of the specially built cupboards that hold many of Joel's tools and equipment.

Below left When Joel and Helena are happy with a design, Joel turns a wooden form on the lathe and they make a plaster mould from it. Here, Helena is pouring slip (liquid clay) into a lampshade mould.

Below right Joel attaches the leg of a Lace bar stool, made from lacey London plane and English ash. The through-tenon joints add strength as well as an attractive design feature.

Opposite The Element pendant combines slip-cast ceramic with a British oak cap and a grey fabric cable.

Left Lightweight, strong, recyclable packaging is an important element of each product's life cycle.

Below left Sponging and smoothing the edges of a piece before the bisque firing.

Below right Finished pieces on display in the Studio Haran office.

Cabbage Blue

For Sarah Johnson, designing and making clothes for her brand, Cabbage Blue, is a constantly evolving learning process. While studying sportswear design at Falmouth University, she found herself drawn to ideas of durability and sustainability, and to natural fabrics such as wool and linen. A postgraduate trip to Japan to learn about indigo dyeing influenced her work greatly. She hand-dyes much of her clothing using either indigo or other natural ingredients, and finds inspiration in the rhythm of the dyeing process, as well as in the raw texture and materiality of cloth and combinations of colour and shape.

While Sarah's clothing may appear simple, her process is intuitive and experimental. She describes it as not always that of the romantic idea of the maker: first staring at the walls, books and imagery, followed by pattern-cutting, stitching, adapting, changing, cutting, stitching again, lots of ironing, a bit of swearing and, finally, photographing. Thinking and looking are vital at every stage; her aim is rawness with an element of resolution. While every piece she creates for commissions and collaborations is different, common features are a sense of purpose and a peaceful, elegantly pared-down form.

Opposite Sarah learnt
the ancient process of
natural indigo dyeing
on a postgraduate
research trip to Japan.

**Above and above
right** Sarah enjoys
the rhythm of indigo
dyeing, a deceptively
simple process that
involves a dye vat,
protective gloves, a
drying line, patience
and a willingness to
experiment.

Opposite In natural, often hand-dyed fabrics, each piece that Sarah makes is different, mapping the constant evolution of her learning process.

Left and below left Sarah works in a light, bright studio in the late-Victorian CAST building in Helston, once part of Cornwall's first secondary school.

Above Each Cabbage Blue piece is unique, hand-made by Sarah from start to finish.

Right While studying sportswear design at Falmouth University, Sarah realised that she was drawn to the wonderful qualities of natural fabric.

Below right Using natural dyes is not always predictable, but does result in an exceptional range of colours. As well as indigo, Sarah has experimented with madder, logwood, walnut husks, eucalyptus and gardenia flowers.

Below left A traditional mannequin – an essential part of Sarah's making process.

Below right Inspiration in various forms, pinned to Sarah's studio wall.

Hannah Batstone

Though hand-crafted using time-honoured, traditional silversmithing and gem-setting techniques, Hannah Batstone's pieces possess a contemporary edge, an organic yet elegant appearance, which sets them distinctly apart. Having grown up making her own jewellery, Hannah moved to Cornwall to study contemporary crafts at Falmouth University, set up her own business afterwards, and now works from a shop-cum-studio on Penryn's historic high street, where she makes and sells her ranges of striking, yet wearable, sterling silver and gold jewellery, and works to commission.

Hannah's aim is to echo the colours, shapes and surfaces she observes in the landscapes around her, from lush woodland to jagged rocks and quarries, with necklaces, bangles, rings, brooches and earrings that bear the subtle marks of the maker's hand. Her designs are often asymmetrical and textured, gently hammered to create ripples that catch the light to create a shimmer, like sunlight glistening on waves. While Hannah enjoys soldering, shaping and forming metal (her father and brother are both metalwork engineers – she thinks there must be something in her genes) her favourite process is working with precious and semi-precious gemstones, which she carefully selects for cut, colour and form. Delicately or deeply coloured, they bring her pieces to life and add a personal, individual quality, as well as confirming their connection to nature.

Opposite Hammering a ring. Surface texture is often an important element of Hannah's pieces.

Above Works in progress are arranged on Hannah's bench.

Left A ring is held in a vice while Hannah collet-sets the gemstone.

Above Hannah's well-organised studio is set up in the back part of her shop.

Left Soldering a ring. Hannah has always enjoyed working with metal.

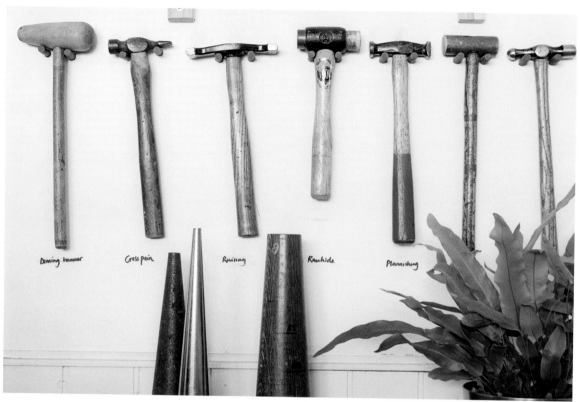

Labels on hammers: Doming hammer · Cross pein · Raising · Rawhide · Planishing

Above Traditional silversmithing makes use of a variety of hammers for different purposes.

Left Hannah's bench, with a clamp holding a ring on which she is presently working.

sit up straight
Shoulders back

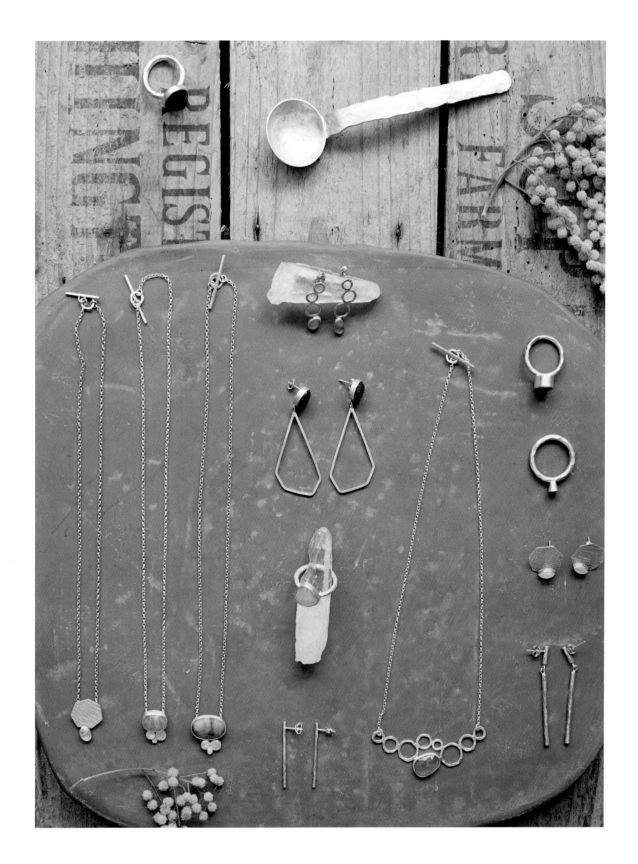

Opposite and above
Hannah makes jewellery in sterling silver and gold, often incorporating precious and semi-precious gems such as sapphires, emeralds, moonstones, topaz and labradorite.

Left One of the display cases in Hannah's shop, on Penryn's Higher Market Street.

Mosevic

Jack Spencer believes that, with a bit of creative thinking, luxury fashion can be designed and made responsibly. A keen kite-surfer and nature-lover, after a degree in 3D design for sustainability at Falmouth University, he began, with a friend, to develop an idea for low-impact, innovative eyewear while working as a freelance product designer. With no office, workshop or backing money, they began to experiment with old jeans and jars of resin, eventually successfully crowdfunding the launch of Mosevic, a range of 'solid denim' eyewear. Jack now runs the business full time from a workshop tucked away in picturesque Ponsanooth, not far from Falmouth.

Mosevic's unique process uses just two raw materials: recycled denim, from manufacturers' excess stock and charity shops, and bio-resin, sourced from waste streams and other industrial processes. The denim is stacked in layers and infused with the resin, then pressed into moulds to cure, so that computer-controlled machinery can cut each piece precisely. These are stone-washed to soften the edges before Jack assembles everything by hand, using high-quality, polarised lenses, brass inlays and five-barrel hinges. The result is a product that is tough and durable yet also lightweight and flexible – and unlike any other sunglasses in the world.

Opposite The unique process of making 'solid denim' sunglasses took Jack years to develop. Here, he wrings excess resin from the layered denim.

Left Each pair of sunglasses is finished by hand. Here, Jack is adjusting the five-barrel hinges.

Below left The wooden moulds. Jack has experimented with a line of phone cases.

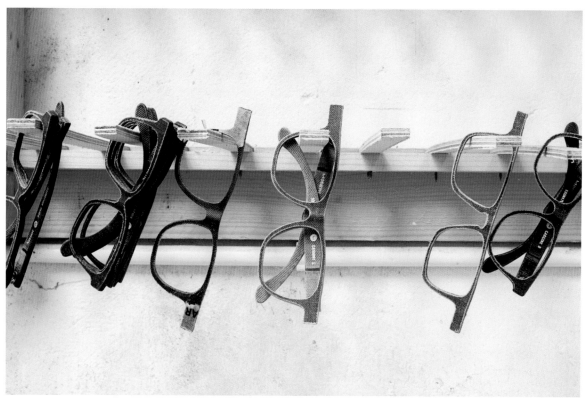

Above and left Recycled jeans of all shapes, sizes and textures are used to make Mosevic sunglasses, so each pair is unique.

Above Powder from the cutting process creates intriguing silhouettes of the hanging arms of sunglasses.

Left The sunglasses are fitted with polarised Zeiss lenses.

The Nature of Paper

It's a testament to how lifelike The Nature of Paper's exquisite paper flowers are that people often pick them up and sniff them. Pam Booth recreates flowers and foliage for floral arrangements and unique, botanical, three-dimensional art works – often in an impressively realistic way, though sometimes as a more abstract interpretation.

Working from the living room of her home in the small city of Truro, Pam needs only a flat surface, a cutting mat and scissors with which to carry out her craft. Though she is trained in graphic design, digital media, animation, art and interior design, her paper floristry is largely self-taught. Everything starts with research. The coastal paths, country hedgerows and sub-tropical gardens of Cornwall provide a huge diversity of plant species that Pam photographs in close up (preferring to leave the real thing for bees, insects and other people to enjoy). She also studies botanical plates and the occasional real flower, which she painstakingly dissects to examine in detail. Having created templates, she then patiently cuts and shapes each individual element, usually by hand, adding colour with paint or pen if needed, before finally constructing the flower on its wire stem and making any final adjustments – a perfectly imperfect representation of nature.

Above Pam doesn't have a garden, but surrounds herself with maintenance-free flowers of all varieties

Left Pam uses different types of paper and card, as well as wire, scissors, punches, ball tools, glue and, sometimes, paints, pastels or ink pens.

Opposite An array of blooms hangs above Pam's desk. Rolls of crepe paper are stored conveniently below.

Debbie Rudolph

Aiming to bring a bold, modern approach to the craft of weaving, Debbie Rudolph explores the colours and textures of the Cornish shorelines and coastlines in her cushions, rugs, wall hangings, bags and scarves. She fell in love with weaving at university, where she studied fashion and textiles, and then, having also trained as a teacher, combined freelance textile design with working in a school part-time. The teaching gradually took over, however, and Debbie spent many years as head of art in a busy inner-city London secondary school, only returning to weaving after she and her husband relocated to Falmouth with their young family.

Debbie works mainly on two large Swedish floor looms in a spacious, light-filled studio that looks out over her garden. The process of constructing woven textiles (both cloth and tapestry) is measured, meditative and, sometimes, back-breaking. Debbie loves every moment of it. Using photographs and drawings as a guide, she sketches out her ideas and spends time carefully combining colours for each piece, then sources the yarn before warping up the loom – which itself can take up to three days. The weaving itself, the exciting part where colours, tones and textures grow together, can develop at, perhaps, a gentle 25cm an hour.

After living in London for so long, Debbie values the beauty of the natural world around her; the flora, fauna, beaches and countryside of Cornwall are a direct inspiration for her designs. She especially enjoys the idea that she is creating something unique, special to the local environment, which will become a cherished part of her customers' everyday lives.

Opposite Debbie uses a wooden winder to load the shuttle with yarn.

Above left Sketches of local landscapes are transformed into carefully colour-coordinated designs for products.

Above right Debbie sets up the loom by passing plain cotton yarn through the heddles to create a warp. The surface weft is all that will eventually be seen.

Above Colours of the sea and shore, evident in these works in progress, are woven on frame looms, which Debbie also uses to teach workshops.

Right The light-filled studio, built by Debbie's husband, looks out over their garden.

Opposite Tapestry weaving on the 1970s Glimakra Swedish tapestry loom. As the yarn is woven over and through the plain cotton warp it creates the surface design.

Left A work in progress, in nature-inspired shades of blue.

Below left Pieces from Debbie's Shoreline collection, inspired by pebbles, sand and sea foam.

Below left Finished
cushions, some striped,
others embellished
with tassels, waiting to
be sent to her gallery
stockists.

Below right Debbie
makes bags and wall
art, as well as cushions,
rugs and scarves.

Opposite Debbie at
work on her 50-year-
old Lillstina four-shaft
loom, which was a
surprise 40th birthday
present from her
husband.

Where to Buy

Alice Selwood
aliceselwood.com
[IG] @alice_selwood
The Poly, Falmouth; thepoly.org

Amy Isles Freeman
amyislesfreeman.co.uk
[IG] @amyislesfreeman

Cabbage Blue
bysarahjohnson.co.uk
The Ottowin Shop, Bristol; ottowinfootwear.co.uk

Debbie Rudolph
debbierudolph.co.uk
etsy.com/uk/shop/StudioRudolph
[IG] @debbierudolph_weaving
Cornwall Crafts Association at Trelissick and
Trelowarren; cornwallcrafts.co.uk
Far and Wild Living, Perranporth;
farandwildliving.co.uk
Jaunty Seagull, Bude; jauntyseagull.co.uk
Penwith Gallery, St Ives; penwithgallery.com

Deer & Shine
deerandshine.com
[IG] @deerandshinejewellery
Market Place Gallery, St Ives;
marketplacegallerystives.co.uk
Newlyn Art Gallery & The Exchange, Penzance;
newlynartgallery.co.uk

Dor & Tan
dorandtan.com (and for stockists)
DOR & TAN, Unit 1, Treglisson Rural Workshops,
Wheal Alfred Road, Hayle

Francli
francli.co.uk (and for stockists)
[IG] @franclicraftwear

Glass by Bryony
glassbybryony.com
[IG] @glassbybryony

Hannah Batstone
hannahbatstone.com
[IG] @hannahbatstonejewellery
The Guild of Ten, Truro; guildoften.com

Juniper Bespoke
juniperbespoke.space
[IG] @junipersees

Kelmi
kelmi.co.uk
[IG] @kelmi_craft
Botanical Atelier, Falmouth; botanicalatelier.co.uk
Potager Garden, nr Falmouth; potagergarden.org

Lancaster & Cornish
lancasterandcornish.com
[IG] @lancasterandcornish
[f] @LancasterandCornish

Miel Studio
mielstudio.co.uk
[IG] @mielstudio.co.uk
Endpaper, Penzance; endpaperandco.com

Mosevic
mosevic.com

Ondine Ash
ondineash.com
[IG] @ondineash
Ondine Ash, Unit 2, Old Brewery Yard, Falmouth

The Nature of Paper
thenatureofpaper.com (and for stockists)
[IG] [f] @thenatureofpaper

Otter Surfboards
ottersurfboards.co.uk
[IG] @ottersurfboards [f] @ottersurf

Paper Birch
paperbirch.co.uk
[IG] @_paper_birch

Pica Pica
etsy.com/uk/shop/picapicadesignco
🔘 @picapica_design

Rose Choules
rosechoulesatelier.com (and for stockists)
🔘 @rosechoules

Sarah Drew
sarahdrew.com (and for stockists)

Sea of Grass
seaofgrass.co.uk
🔘 @seaofgrassstudio
Artisan, Tremenheere Sculpture Gardens, Gulval
🔘 @artisan.tremenheere
Botanical Atelier, Falmouth; botanicalatelier.co.uk
Botany, Clapton, London; botanyshop.co.uk

Studio Haran
studioharan.co.uk
The workshop at Devichoys Farm, Perranarworthal
(open by appointment, tel 07827 603808)

Tinkebu
tinkebu.com
🔘 @tinkebucornwall

Wendy Wilbraham
🔘 @wendyjwilbraham
Beside the Wave, Falmouth; beside-the-wave.co.uk
Collate Interiors, Axminster; collateinteriors.com
FED 303, Bristol; 🔘 @fed.303
Newlyn Art Gallery & The Exchange, Penzance;
newlynartgallery.co.uk
No. 56, Penzance; no-56.com
The Old Coastguard Hotel, Mousehole;
oldcoastguardhotel.co.uk
Penwith Gallery, Saint Ives; penwithgallery.com
The Poly, Falmouth; thepoly.org
Ryder&Hope, Lyme Regis; ryderandhope.com

Acknowledgements

We would like to thank the following people who were invaluable in helping us to publish Make: Cornwall:

Peggy Sadler, not only for being a superb designer but who was also a fount of knowledge and wisdom, who sorted out the printing and other logistics, and was enormously patient with us. We honestly couldn't have done it without her.

Ben Mostyn, talented photographer (and Anya's husband) who shot our landscapes, created fabulous video footage of the makers and was generally a pillar of support.

Emma Kerswell of Seabord Creative, for crafting a professional social media campaign for us. She's amazing.

John Boyle and Fionn Crow of Crow Creative, who edited such a wonderful video to help with our crowdfunding campaign.

Alice Selwood, who patiently spent a Sunday afternoon modelling for a cover that we ended up not using. Seasalt Cornwall, who so kindly provided clothes for the shoot at short notice. (And Maddison, who lent us her phone case.)

Krystal Fanning, aka Paper Birch, who designed our beautiful cover.

Cultivator Cornwall and the IoS Growth Fund for their professional support, and A2F for the grant towards our crowdfunding campaign.

Kelvin Harrow, who built the set for the cover that was not to be.

SUPPORTERS
Newlyn Art Gallery & The Exchange
Duchy of Cornwall Nursery
Cornwall Contemporary, Penzance
Christine Nullmeyers
Lancaster & Cornish
Breeze Art & Makers CIC
Morva Marazion
Circa 21, Penzance
Georgina Pickworth
Clementine Nield
Nick Rudlin
Helena Cochran
Elaine and Jim Miles
Kelmi